waterways books

WOMAN
selected poems

releasing new voices, revealing new perspectives

WOMAN

waterways
an imprint of flipped eye publishing
www.flippedeye.net

First printed in 2003
Copyright © Agnes Meadows 2003
Reprinted 2005, 2007, 2009, 2012
Cover Design © Petraski, flipped eye publishing, 2005

'There Is That Place', 'Dancer', 'Seasons', 'Tracy Says', 'I Got The Auchen Toshen Blues', 'You And Me', and 'In My Heaven' have previously been published in You And Me. © Agnes Meadows.

'Hagia Sofia', and 'Quantum Love' have previously been published in Quantum Love © Agnes Meadows.

'When I Die' was translated in Arabic and published in the Palestinian PEN Anthology 2000

'View From A Moving Train' has previously been published in The Oak King (A London Voices Anthology)

ISBN: 0-9542247-1-X

This book is dedicated my Mum, who made me strong.

WOMAN
selected poems

Agnes Meadows
2003

WOMAN
selected poems

CONTENTS

THERE IS THAT PLACE

There is that place
Just below his ear
At the base of his neck, beneath the hairline,
The hair just long enough to curl like a child's fingers onto his waiting skin,
Calling out for lips to smooth away his desperation.
And I am there to answer that call.

There is that place
Along the forearm
Between wrist and elbow
Which begs for the touch of my fingertips,
Keeping me awake in the long afternoons
With the heat penetrating my skin like warm summer sun on ripe fruit,
Cherries, peaches, pomegranates...
He is a generous lover
Who brings me gifts of roses wrapped in vine leaves,
Red geraniums,
Honey dripping from the comb.

There is that place
At the edge of his mouth
Where lips curl into easy laughter,
Smile an ocean wide exposing the pleasure of his soul spent in endless
        days
By seas as vast as turquoise eternity,
No one running faster than the racing heartbeat,
Lips betraying the ache,
The hunger... the hunger...

There is that place
In his eyes
Silence speaking of need or forgotten dreams.
He does not have to say a single word,
Not one word,
For the pen has written deep words there already,
No cracks in his composure exposed
Until the gentle daybreak.

There is that place
At the base of his throat
Where the skin sits in simple folds
Like silk under my hand,
Deep desire in the undone days.
It sings out for my breath
Running the tidal dance of things he does not know he wants,
Salt rising to the surface
Removed by my mouth,
Only my mouth.
What could be simpler than the solution I offer for this season?
For this poor season,
Not running more than a moon-rise,
Not more than a handful of weeks
Between peacock pleasure and the first rain of autumn.

There is that place
Where cheek meets temple
And the body's moisture collects in a stream of knowledge.
And other people always calling his name,
Never a minute to sit,

Feel the threatening tiredness lifting like a smile in the morning,
Brighter than any tasted treasure,
Absorbing life or the absence of darkness.

There is that place
Under his strong brown fingers,
Burning an embrace across my aching limbs,
Feeling the blood dart like a coursing hare across the hollow hills,
Chasing away betrayal, cut down to the very bone.
His hands, like a net,
Catching what cannot be acknowledged in any human heart,
Transforming it to gold, or amethysts, or pearls,
His refusal better than promises,
Or payment for kindness yet to be given.

There is that place
In the turn of his body.
Imagination runs riot,
And I am burned to cinders.

DANCER

She's sari'd, worried, domestically buried.
She's curried, harried, good arrangement married.
She's unconnected, unprotected, discounted,
Each and every damn night mounted.
Pinned, maligned, assigned, more sinned against than sinning,
Contained, restrained, not a single day of winning.
She's
Invisible, derisible, cost too high so feelings inadmissible,
Glassed up, passed up, passed by, can't cry.
(Not in public anyway).
She's
Demure, obscure, never lost that Eastern promise in her eyes
    allure,
Monitored, barometered, emotionally manicured,
Dreams jaded, life faded, no way out, will die like this unaided.
She's - wounded, hounded, heart and blood impounded,
Off the wall, rice and dhal, different cultural protocol,
Circumscribed, Bindi-tied, body bruises allibied,
Injected, subjected, never raising voice inflected,
Wear and tear, mute to fear, over-wrought and over here.

But,
At night,
She is - Ravana, the Demon,
Who eats his children without thought.

And,
At night,
She is - Kali, the Destroyer,
Swimming in an ocean of blood.

And,
At night,
She is - Radha,
Waiting for her lover with jasmine in her hair.

And,
At night,
She is - Krishna,
Who lifts the flute of the Universe to his lips.

And,
At night,
She is - Durga,
Who gives birth to time in her dark womb.

And,
At night,
She is - Shiva,
Dancing...until the end... of the world.

THESE SHOES
(A pair of red shoes with 2-foot heels)

These shoes are *not* for walking in!
These shoes are traffic lights, an idling sign,
The equivalent of neon flashing red lights along my instep
Signalling
"Stop!
"Start!
"Stop!
"Start!
"Stop....start!"
You'd have to be dead to misinterpret the sub-text.

If I were Carmen Miranda,
I'd be *dancing* in these shoes,
Shoulders shaking,
Big Cuban 'come-on' smile water meloning my face,
Rhythm in my feet saying
"Aqui hombre, aqui...por favor."

If I were Monroe,
I'd be *standing* in these shoes,
Standing with my skirts billowing from the updraft,
And that look in my eyes,
Half closed against the night heat,
Leaving you in little doubt what might
Cool me down.

If I were Madonna,
I'd be *singing* in these shoes,
Mouth slipping in and out of "Yes!"

Body running the slow marathon of wild approval,
Sweat falling like amber onto the ground,
Rough appetite worked up right from my bones,
Giving it everything I got.

If I were Cleopatra,
I'd be *resting* in these shoes,
Laying back against the scarlet cushions,
Breathing the Nile darkness,
Asp hidden for now from the Egyptian evening,
And Mark Anthony would have his hand
On my heel.

No,
These shoes are definitely *not* for walking in!
They're for giving you messages
You can only take
Laying down.

SEASONS

When frost crisps holly,
And December streets are washed with empty sleet,
Or grey-lace rain, which blankets years of bleak neglect,
I will love you warm as mulled-wine bruising, and the smell of clove or
        cinnamon within the orange curling flame.
When winter's berry gladdens hearts,
And wren and robin shrill cold season's keys to open Christmas gates,
And carol singers breathe the happy verse of Yuletide promises
        into the ice-silvered night,
And snow erases footsteps as we stumble, wintry kiss content,
Through time's dimmed passageways into another diamond day,
Know I will love you sweet as wild, long notes held captive
        in the last beguiling moment of the dying Holly King.

When buds and bees both seize the April hour,
And Earth's blood hums in tribal resurrection all along the skein of pagan
        crested hills
Fresh white and feathered as a shining swan,
I will love you fierce as passing tempests which quick draw breath, then
        throw down rain as pearls before in haste they move along.
When vernal feasting beckons, sly
Through trees which reach in blossom-fingered press on branches long
        before the cherry fruit has grown,
And Maypole's keening for those Gods which grew with ivy stillness
        on the decorated bough
Beribboned wishes sealing spring's great pleasure in the enduring knot
        of birth,
Through all of this, my dark unbridled darling,
Know I will love you joyful as the play of merry children rolled like eggs
        from Easter's happy hands.

When crickets chant through yellow leaf,
And summer dances on the stage of drowsy fruitfulness until it's bare-
      legged caught in rosy afternoons,
And Oak King strokes the vibrant blooms awake to gilded acorn coupling,
I will love you slow as sun-stained dreams, which snooze
      among the dappled under-growth,
Their scent imbued with heat, and hay, and untamed honey heaviness.
When mid-year riches hurly burly from the shell of life,
And all the grapes, which run along the vine, have burned their hearts
      with busy Bacchus truths,
And insects settle in the mellow dust in unstung lazy symphony,
Or corn grows ripe beneath the cap of onion-layered skies
Replete with sparrows spilling out their rhyme to clean the sin of secret
      apple cheer,
Know I will love you firm as stones which stand appliquéd on unmoving
      August views, each turret misted with the mottled moss of dusk.

When pumpkins roar in spectral nights,
And bonfires hurl their screeching offspring high into the velvet void
      with bursting rocket shout,
And sunlight fades earth's scarlet avalanche of leaves to burn
      the fingers of a waning world,
I will love you calm as trees which stand unflinching down the passing
      cavalcade of years,
and keep their silent term of dryad touch locked tight in timbered hearts.
When autumn's blood has coloured heath,
And harvest dims the favoured clocks whose tick spurs men to martial
      weariness,
And seagull's raucous tumble follows plough, or vixens bark at men
      from hollowed logs where toadstools snore,
There, soft within October's yielding grip, where every contour's smudged
      or rain beclouded dim,

And every drop of warmth is squeezed at last from flame-enameled air,
Know I will love you long as sight, your name in every stalk and blade,
until time's very blankness dulls the mind, or rubs out hope,
Or I am dogwatch done.

WHEN I DIE

When I die
I want you to ring bells
And cover the pavements in rose petals, frozen frangipani leaves,
White, white lilac, and dandelion spears,
So that wherever you walk it will be a celebration.

When I die
I want you to play loud music.
Anything with drums,
Or the artist formerly known as Prince,
Or guitars deep on base-line
Along with heavy dancing,
Thighs Velcro'd together, skin itching with effort,
So that every time you feel the hungry chill across your shoulders that
        comes with good sound,
You'll think of me and smile.

When I die
I want you to shoal up my friends,
Net them all up.
Get them drunk with memories and fifty-year-old Malt,
And each one has to tell a story with me as the punch-line, just like my
        life;
Laughter always easy on our lips
When we lay on those Greek beaches, gilding our lucid fantasies,
Or sat in darkened theatres afraid to cry in case we'd never stop,
Or held each other as sisters, knowing that at least would never go away.
Then maybe my passion will still echo in your head.

When I die
I want you to catch the rain from Spring mornings
In blue glass bottles,
Line them up on a shelf somewhere very still
Where they'll gather no dust,
And watch their shadows juggle on the waiting wall amidst the spiders.
Then, whenever there's a storm,
Or the daytime quiet's riven by the sound of water running,
Or you see a waving web,
You'll remember the colour of my eyes.

When I die
I want you to go shopping
Big time... big time!
Buy three of everything in different colours, none of them matching,
Blister the plastic 'til you're all stored out,
Significant attention driving salesgirls crazy, and pay for it all in pennies
So they'll have to count each one at a time.
Then when anyone lays into chic speak,
Or you're lost amongst the mirrors and the silks,
You'll still have my pleasure to trade in.

When I die
I want you to watch every Star Trek movie ever made.
Twice.
So that when you look up into that unused sky
Especially at night when it's all stitched up with stars
And the moon makes you shiver with cold, dead as old love,
And all your time's your own,
You'll know I'm buzzing round there, Worf-factor nine...
Still making it so.

VIEW FROM A MOVING TRAIN

(England, August 2000)

Here sycamores march along the dusty lanes,
Rose Bay Willow Herb crowding sleepy railway banks,
Trains worming over hills maggotted with sheep
Or the bold embroidery of cows and pylons.

Here dog-eyed daisies growl,
And bindweed runs nettled through crammed black bramble sweetness,
And hay spins, baled and ready for collection,
Tired in August's easy symmetry,
Regimented in runnels soft as Offa's Dyke.

Mute, the scarlet harvester spills its iron heart upon the ground,
Men sitting by in loose-limbed company,
Saying little,
For theirs is the conversation of seasons not moments,
Sandwiches like church steps ready for eating
Under a blue paintbrush sky.

Rivers run the gauntlet of fresh curried fields
Where plough has stitched together early autumn harvest,
And church's spires thrust aglow with honeycombed light
Sticky with faith and morning sun,
Capturing a broo-brooding of pigeons
And Mountain Ash berries rowaning their bush afire.

Above bridges and wheat fields,
Over firs and drowsing oaks,
Birds pierce sky-crumb scattered clouds,

A froth of starlings,
An eddy of nightingales,
An invasion of crows,
A steeple of ravens
Or sparrows' crosspatch chatter,
A semaphore of feathers.

And the Oak King smoothes down his foliate face,
Kisses the earth with green abandon,
Yawning in hammer-dryad sleep,
Another year's relentless slip holding him fast.

TRACY SAYS

Tracy says her parents are getting a divorce.
There's someone else, she says, her Mam's been seeing, and now
    she's leaving them behind.

And Tracy says I'm lucky.
That my Mam's always home to make things nice for all of us,
And *she'd* never go to the pub on Fridays and come back drunk and say
    her husband was a loser,
Or make him cry when he thought no one else was listening.

And Tracy says my life is easy.
I never have to wear my sister's clothes like she does,
Or pawn the wedding rings just to pay the rent,
Or eat beans-on-toast for Sunday dinner and pretend to like it
When the dole runs out.

And Tracy says I've got no worries,
That *my* Dad's clever, with a job in an office in town,
Which makes Christmases and birthdays proper parties
With candles and ribbons and carols round the Christmas tree,
And presents that don't come from Woollies, and the paper's new
    each time.

And Tracy says she's jealous, even though she's my best friend,
And I'm better than her sister,
And she wishes she could come and live with me
So she wouldn't have to share a bedroom any more,
And we could get a dog together, and call him Philip like her baby
    brother who died.

I told her, even though my Mam makes the best spaghetti in the world,
And I've got a TV in my bedroom, and there's a garden out back
      with a swing in it my Dad put up for me,
And I've got trainers that say Nike all up the sides,
I told her, she wouldn't like it much in our house if she lived there.
But Tracy says I'm lying.

And Tracy says she's going to find another best friend
Unless I invite her home for tea more often.
But I can't because my Dad says we have to get his permission before
      we can ask anyone home,
And he doesn't really like Tracy 'coz she's a slut, he says.

And Tracy says I'm being silly when I tell her I don't ever want to marry.
But if I do, my husband won't shout at me or slap my face
And then tell people I've fallen over in the bath because I'm clumsy.
And he won't shut the door on my fingers 'by mistake' so they broke
      if I didn't iron his shirts quite right.

And if I had a boyfriend, he'd never tell me to sit quietly and not
      contradict him
Because I'm wasting God's good air by breathing.
And, unless it's winter, I won't wear dresses with long sleeves
Like Mam does when Dad's given her what she deserves.
(But she says he doesn't mean it really, coz he loves us).
And I don't ever want to be in love
If it means I have to pretend to be stupid
Just to keep the peace.

And Tracy says she thinks my Dad's amazing.

But I prefer hers any day

Because he makes me laugh, and I don't have to pay for it afterwards,

And he listens when I'm scared that Freddy Kruger's in the wardrobe

(Even though I know he isn't really).

And I wouldn't mind the beans-on-toast, or not having a dog called Philip,

If I could just feel safe.

But Tracy says I'm daft.

ABSOLUTELY LAST POEM TO A PAST LOVE

(London, August 2000)

In Winter's cloudburst
We dodged raindrops
Like we dodged love.

So I found another umbrella
Under which to splash
Singing, Gene Kelly style.

Now even the rain feels warm.

I GOT THE AUCHEN TOSHAN BLUES

I got the Auchen Toshan Blues.
31 years in the cask and full of fire.
Soooo smooth,
Like the voice of God on my lips.

When I saw you there,
Dark brown bond
Making my head spin at the thought
Of how you'd feel in my mouth
I knew even then, there was no turning back.
Rough charm? You have no rough charm.
Just sweeeeet undertones
Strong
As any strong
Young man
Wrapping himself around you
Whispering
Whispering
Promises
He knows he cannot keep.

I got the Auchen Toshan blues,
Never tasted anything like the body of you - ooh, ooh
No matter what the cost, I'll pay the price,
A pound for every note of peat, salt, honey and heather.
Amber dreams swallowed quickly,
Before they
Evaporate.

You can sing to me
In your
Triple
Distilled
Voice.
Liquid love.

I got the Auchen Toshan Blues.
Never smelled your equal.
Low-land bouquet leaves me undone.
Slow trail across my body.
You leave a mark on my soul. Cannot be erased.
But you're no child, 31 years waiting and filled with darkness.
You give yourself to everyone – yet I cannot walk away.
So, I'll just be
Waiting
Waiting
Knowing I won't forget you
Filling me
Filling me
Up
Again.
Yea... yea...

What do you see?
When you look at me, what
Do you see?

Do you see an
Easy smiling
Easy laughing
Easy living
Easy loving
        woman?

Do you see a
Low morals
Low Church
Low fidelity
Low expectation
Low feeling, low price, low flying
        woman?

Do you see a
Bad blood
Bad ass, bad mouth
Bad news
Bad apple, bottom of the barrel, worm in her heart
Bad vibrations
        woman?

Is that what you see
When you look at me?

Yea... well, maybe I'm some of those things.
Hell... maybe I'm all of those things.
But let me tell you, what you see is NOT what you get.

'Cos I'm a
High tech
High heeled
High maintenance
High as a kite
High bred, high kicking,
Hi, how ya doin', have a nice day
                              woman.

And I'm a
Strong minded,
Strong jawed, strong-armed,
Strong blooded, strong willed
Triple strength, subtle and multi-layered
Strong principled,
Stronger than the cause that binds you
Stronger than the curse that blinds you
                              woman.

And I'm a hard up, hard headed,
Hard working, hard playing,
Hard knock School of Life,
Hard bargaining, hard listening,
Hard done by,
Hardly worth talking about how often I sung the blues
Then hard rocked back to freedom
                              woman.

And I'm a big hipped,
Big mouth, big impact, big word,
Big Smoke, big breakfast,
Big storm brewing, lock up your sons,
Big bite, chew gum at the same time as walking
Big dream
          woman.

Yea, I'm a BIG dream woman.
I don't deal in skinny dreams.

'Cos I'm a sharp shootin'
Sharp talkin',
Sharp dressin',
Sharp as a razor
Sharp enough to cut you
Sharp eyed
          woman.

And I'm a finger lickin' good news, good looking,
Time off for good behaviour
Good sense
Good God, good grief,
Good morning and good night,
Good Golly Miss Molly rock 'n' roll and
Good sound
          woman.

So next time you see me,
Take a good hard look.
Spend some time thinking about it,

Open your eyes
And don't leave your brain behind.

'Cos I'm a fast flowing
Smooth talking, slow moving,
Mother, sister, lover, wife,
Got here before you,
Still be staying when you're long gone,
Fierce fighting,
Beat me with your fists, can't bend me
Totally
Unbreakable
                    woman!

"You're useless! Do you hear me. A useless little bitch! Jesus Christ,
if you died tomorrow, nobody would miss you, you know that. Get out of
my sight! I can't stand looking at you."

She stood there, face a locked door,
Just taking it, no chance to even up the score.
Taking it, because there was nothing else to do,
Because that's the way it was,
Because she simply had to.
Because there was no alternative,
Because her life was all give.
Because she was powerless, featureless,
The meeker sex, uniquer sex,
The 'beat-'em-hard' ensuring they're the weaker sex.
Because she had nothing to say, had lost the will,
Lacked the strength, and lacked the skill.
Because her pride had been eco-vandalised,
Brutalised, misogynised and paralysed.
Because for her, pride didn't come before the fall,
For her, pride didn't come at all.
Because her timing was bad,
Wrong hour, wrong place.
Because she'd 'grown accustomed to his face'.
Because he could, and would, and had, and did,
Because the system was to blame, he said.
Because she'd had to rough it up, tough it up,
Never-known-a-day-when-there's-enough it up.
Because she was fair game,
Because the government's to blame.
Because God is dead, the King is dead, Diana's dead, the dog is dead,

And there's a war amongst the Heavenly hierarchy,
Because we have a monarchy.
Because she has no future,
Because *he* has no future,
Because there's no future in futures.
Because we've seen the end of rock'n'roll,
Because he's never, ever come off the dole.
Because he 'just wanted to be free',
Yea... so did she.
Because it was hot, because it was cold,
Because, for Christ's sake, she was only 8 years old.

Abuse is a chain which leaves an ache.
You are what you hate.
You are what you hate.
You are what you hate.

BANANAS
To a Taxi Driver from Afghanistan

"In my garden there were roses,
And each morning I would play Brahms in the shadows of mulberry trees.
My wife, my children, would sit and listen.
It gave them pleasure."

He was a little man, smile a crescent moon,
The hair on the back of his hands sprung to attention like an army of eager
                                                    recruits,
His accent, thick as butter spread on new baked bread,
Requiring meticulous concentration,
Warm nuggets of words to be swallowed carefully.
Shabby jacket belied seams of cultured richness,
A hidden master load,
Quick intelligence lighting his eyes,
Easy to miss in glib assumption of Occidental supremacy;
He was, after all, just another immigrant cabby,
Delivering pizza's on the side to make ends meet,
Mean shoes and meaner London life still better than his ravaged Kabul
                                                    yesterdays.

As we talked, my attention wriggling worm-like on the hook of his
                                                    memories,
A life I could not imagine was spread before me,
                a foreign carpet of warp and weft exotica where I would
                always be the stranger feasting
                        in arcane comfort
While all around me others fed on bitter flesh.

He described the years he'd spent studying music in Moscow,
Mozart, Brahms, Rachmaninov roaring through the Russian winter days
Waiting to slip out of his hands, run out of his fingers, jubilant with
                                                    freedom,
Resonating his inner dream of plenty.

And then the fundamental madness which crushed bright hope,
Afghani conversion by bearded men who'd shoot at clouds,
Put out the very light of expectation,
Lock up their daughters in blind anthropomorphic faith,
Narrowing every act to cold corruption,
Even women eating bananas illegalised, become somehow obscene.
The Prophet's prodigal sons wasting abundance,
Taliban faith replacing reason,
Conversion by Kalishnikov;

'They burned my music, saying it was a sin against God,
My home, children, my very life gone up in smoke."
His voice held no reproach, just a statement of fact,
Humility torched, dignity denied.
"What kind of God would need to see my music burned," he asked,
"Would trash my sons,
See filth in women eating fruit?"

    Rhetorical questions. I could only nod agreement, shamed by what I
        took for granted
            every day.

"If I won the Lottery," he grinned at last,
"I would buy a piano,
Find a garden with mulberry trees.
Buy my wife bananas."

BY THE BOSPHORUS
8 May

The husband I had loved for years sat before me smiling,
Rolling out histories I had not shared,
Successes I had not witnessed,
New love pleasures unknown to me.
I did the same.
It felt comfortable, companionable,
Joining us not with betrayal, but with a web of laughter.

We walked slowly by the Bosphorus, its silver breath a fitting backdrop,
Watching Spring unfurl like a shy child.

And when we said goodbye, we knew
That was just the start of it.

HAGIA SOFIA

You have woken my heart, human,
When I have been asleep.

It is Spring, and the earth is warm.
Everywhere the Mother reaches upward,
A girl crowned with jasmine and foxgloves,
Imam echoes colouring bright vision,
The Golden Horn, the blue Bosphorus
Bound in chains from continent to continent.
They have always been there.
I have always been there.
Blood is in my bricks, spilled on the stones, which hold my heart.
I remember each drop, each sacrifice,
The cry of women,
The wailing of the lost and faithless standing
In wonder beneath the canopy of faith.

I am old as the Old Woman,
Older than towns or bridges,
Older than men's memory, or writing on walls
Which point direction for brash young men when they are eager
                                    to leave their mark on eternity's dark page.

Once I was beautiful.
Kings trembled at my beauty,
Sacrificed children in my name,
Went to war,
Came home crippled and afraid for love of me.
When I stood up in the morning, surrounded by sunlight,
Paradise alive in every gleaming shaft,

They could not look at me without weeping.

I grew heavy with worship,
A thousand thousand candles lit for me every hour,
Gold brazen as Heaven's eyes wreathing my limbs.
Men wooed me with a lover's kiss,
Covered me with silk and soft words.
Conquerors riding from the endless East, gory with victory,
Their wild white horses covered in sapphires and silver,
Begged my forgiveness,
Covering their foreheads with dust as a sign of humility before God.

I forgave them,
Forgetting their names in an instant.

Now beauty has passed,
Age's silent wisdom atrophies in stone.
Emperors have come and gone,
Their wives and children scurrying into the groaning stillness.
Each one scratches their name onto my skin
In case they are forgotten too swiftly,
Each one carries the poor burden of humanity.
Time passes slowly.
I remain alone, the rock upon which those burdens crack and split,
The inconsequentialities of man become blatant.
I remain alone, the closing of an eye,
Timeless as yellow hills or passing seasons,
Whispering... centuries... millennia...
Whispering... sleeping... stronger than bridges.
Time passes... slowly.
I remain.

SHARK ATTACK
January 2001

Whenever you leave the room
I am torn in half
Soul torn
Limbless
A shark attack of emptiness
Desire shoaling around me in neon bites.

I net your eyes for moments,
Drowning,
Then watch them swim away,
Schooled to circumspection.

My mouth surfs yours
In a rock pool of longing,
Skin hungers for skin,
Even the air between us fretting
Like a bag-full of catfish
Craw-daddying up to the surface of calm,
Ignoring Hammerhead tradition.

FROG

He was not beautiful!
Even after I had kissed him, he was not what one would call exactly
    beautiful.
His dishevelled face was a patchwork quilt sewn together carelessly,
A bland rainbow of features, frayed and unravelling,
Blinking against that lustrous halo of magical intervention,
His body comfortable as an old mattress.
Nothing exceptional anywhere.

Perhaps my expectations had been too high.
Perhaps what I wanted was impossible;
Someone a little more conducive,
More compatible with my personal circumstances.

I believed my Mother when she told me all Princes were handsome.
It went with the territory, she said, along with honour and affluence.
She only wanted the best for me, she said,
Someone of the right calibre, to give me the life I deserved,
Keep me in the manner to which *she* would rapidly become
    accustomed.

So I kissed him,
Dismissing tales of warts as hearsay,
Concentrating on the task at hand,
Puckering my lips so small, physical contact was minimal...
The most unromantic, least passionate kiss imaginable.

It seemed to do the trick.

After the transformation, it would be untrue to say I was disappointed.
When I first saw him, I felt nothing at all
Having been trained well in the art of self-containment.
He was, after all, immensely wealthy.
I would have a comfortable life.
I would be taken care of.
Mother would be proud of me.
I kept my face straight, displaying nothing,
No emotion... nothing.
I had fulfilled my part of the bargain.
The spell was, after all, broken.

And then he smiled.

It was like dawn breaking through darkness,
The widest, most crooked wrinkle of a smile,
Illuminating everything,
Turning that blank window of a face into a panorama filled with warmth
        and brilliance,
Transforming him like magic into a different being,
Turning me inside out, and upside down.

There was a silence about him,
A tragic loneliness, which splintered the heart and made you review
        everything you had ever learned about enchantment.
A passive strength radiated from that impossible smile,
Not like stones, for they are unyielding,
But like forests, or the balance of things *embracing you*.
He played with nobility like cat and cricket,
Leaving you gasping with the fire of it.
Hungry as a pauper's child waiting to be fed.

He smiled, and reeled me in on his eyes,
Green as ivy, as jade, or trees in July leaf or water in the lily pond,
Hooking me like a resisting salmon on the upstream journey home.

I wanted to swim into him,
Reach out to touch that unremarkable face,
Claim him like an undiscovered country of which no maps had ever
        been drawn,
Leave my mark upon him
So there could never be doubt as to who was possessor or who was
        possessed.

He smiled and said my name,
Wrecking me on the uncurrented waters of his voice,
Face tranquil and clear despite everything,
Pool calm, though I was churning in anguish.

He smiled and moved forward to hold me,
Immobilising me with his potency,
A captive charmed by powers gripping me fiercer than ogres.

Things moved on quickly after that,
And it's been a while since I've thought of Mother.
There hasn't been time...
Life
Has been
Too rich.

Beneath the roots of lilies,
Under grappling, slithering weed flow,
In green light rippled and tremulous with September's failing sun,
Laced by dragonfly wings, crack willow,
Fire on the water willow-the-wisp,
Leg froth of water boatmen,
With eels wriggling in reeds brown-topped by starlings and high voiced
           pipistrel shrieking,
We would sit and sing, he and I,
Sit and sing, the water around us flat as a mirror,
Silent as hidden heartbeats,
Mist skittering and tearing from bank to bank,
We would sing, he and I,
Arias fashioned from dusk's grape-dark shadows,
Constellation's chorus batted from his throat to mine, and back.
To and fro,
To and fro,
Knee deep in resonance,
Knee deep, knee deep, knee deep in resonance.

Gentle as a moth at midnight
He would touch me with his eyes,
Curl his limbs round mine, warm and long as a season of harvests
           spread out to dry,
Then leap skyward, gazelle swift, heart's wealth exposed,
Electrified and with the grace of angels,
Rising, a moon gilded arrow fletching old summer's sensual fervour,
Arcing through the twilight in a scatter of silver droplets.

Green, green the light on his body,
Dancing through monkey flower, reed mace and purple agrimony,
Lithe as a swan consumed by the ripe hand of sunset.

Green, green the light on his body,
Uneasy my glance that followed his going,
My heart a bed of roses in which he was the greatest thorn.

But if he had kissed me just once,
If he had looked more deeply into my spell-bedazzled face,
Seen the charm-wrapped gifts waiting to be laid bare,
A transformation wrought by love alone
Piercing as a bramble or any forest adder's sting...
If he had kissed me just once
Softening the sorcery that held me captive,
Releasing me from bondage,
Oh I would at least have known the touch of him,
Just once,

Something to warm my senses,
Necklace my mind with memories.
It would have been enough to engineer change,
And turn the faery clocks back
To the time when love was a possibility.

Now I sit amongst the stones weakened with longing,
My love a wild bird caught in the net of his mouth,
Carrying a burden of loneliness so heavy it makes me unrecognisable.
Winter's bleak coat is shaken out again, ready for use,
Skies become noisy with migration,

The water grows cold, numbing my voice.
Sometimes we lay under the lake's frozen surface for days, immobilised
by ice and February harshness.

There is no going back.

YOU AND ME - Remembering Mexico

Miguel-Angel - where are you?
Winging across that dusty Mexican valley,
Stars over dead volcano days,
No dark lover, but a man of integrity, dealing in Disney dreams,
While pyramids crumbled in the hungry snake-filled dawn,
Kingfisher blues hovered in the blazing jacaranda,
You and me, jaguar hunting of the heart.

Joselito - where are you?
Through the Zona Rosa like a brother,
Driving your red Mustang those summer nights.
And we'd be laughing, you and me, laughing at the tricks we'd played
      like dumb children,
Giving the hard word to low-brow policemen who'd devour dollars from
      your waiting fingers, like jackals who'd been starved one day
      too long.
You and me, not seeing the danger as we'd change gears along paesano
      routes,
Crickets singing in the muddled gutters,
And I'd forget about the London longing for a while, singing along
      with Cocker,
Very loud, his loss-filled voice grating.
And you and me, we'd look soft in the Azteca darkness,
Your hair curling in sleep on pale crushed sheets,
And my fingers sticky with secret loving.

Manolo - where are you?
Hollow laughter tearing up the winter silence,
Moth filled epicentre of my young girl, nighttime talking,
You and me arguing about art, and life, and how it would never be better,

Around us the stones collecting secrets, holding on to them, like rain
        in puddles without rainbows,
For all the rainbows had been gifted already,
Given away,
Wrapped carefully, then torn open and forgotten,
The Cuernavaca sunrise leaving us bruised and sad,
You and me watching the roaches samba across my kitchen floor,
And you grinning as you chased them out, broom held high
        like a weapon of doom for small creatures,
And me wanting to see you laugh more often.

Luis - *mi alma*, where are you?
Life's breath breathing, *vida de mi vida*,
Soul love buried, buried so deep,
Afraid of the anguish I'd feel again if I freed you from the small space
        where you've been hoarded all these years.

You and me catching the jazz in the Mariachi string beat,
Wild harp guitaring through those dust-filled low streets
Swept clean in the September storms, rain so heavy you couldn't see
        beyond your outstretched hands,
Grey as your eyes, grey as leaving, grey as the breath of Indians dead
        now for long, long years,
Malachite dreams crushed with time wasted in Tlaloc's fierce embrace.

You and me reading stories of the Revolution, dead heroes,
        whose names brought tears to your eyes,
But left me wasted, for I had my own revolution to deal with.

You and me walking through the scarlet hibiscus,
Palms edging powder sand, scorpions and kites playing games,
And winds silencing any doubts I had,

The best of times, the worst of times,
Mamacita catcalls fraying my patience at the edges,
Those dream factory images playing across our internal screens.

You and me laying in that stolen bed, where you'd taken carnations from
        the garden so I wouldn't wake alone,
Covering my body with flower petals,
Licking the dew off the leaves,
Where the pleasure was so intense I thought I'd die of it,
And you said you'd die anyway,
So I had to walk away in case it killed me outright.

We seized time as if we were immortal,
Passion knitted into the warp and weft of days, and weeks,
Years of life,
An endless ribbon snaking out, until the loom became invisible.

At night the churchyard was filled with candles,
Roses cascading from an Indian heaven into cathedrals filled with gold,
        and light, and loving,
Foreign angels and saviours absorbing the darkness,
Like you and me for that sweet present.

LOVE AT A DISTANCE – May 2002

You call me wife sometimes,
Always late at night when nobody is listening.
We both know it's safer like that,
Because if they knew you loved me all hell would break loose.
I think that Hell is a territory we're both familiar with
'Tho we've entered its domain by different doors.

I sit crowded by emptiness,
My heart entangled with yours, like brambles on the ground.
Where we fitted together so perfectly,
Your body into mine,
Now there is only space,
The puzzle we had both thought complete now unfinished,
That vital final piece gone missing.
And I know you suffer as I do, gouged equally by thorns of longing,
Watchful and over-patient until you become suffocated with waiting.
I do not have a patent on loneliness,
But at least I have the luxury of tears
Whereas you have no such comfort,
And even happiness is considered self-indulgence.

We make plans.
I imagine you next to me, arguing or sleeping,
Safe, nightmare free.
We fit together like spoons, smooth and flawless,
No longer having to be polite, just easy in each other's company,
Silence no longer a threat
But merely something couples share when they're untroubled.

I imagine day after day of you without goodbyes entering the picture,
Without pretence colouring our emotions,
Or fear stalking every single thing we do ready to consume us.

One day, we say, it will be different,
Torturing ourselves with the uncertainty of when.
You say that when this is all over,
You will compensate me for everything, all the disappointments and
                betrayals of my life,
That you will be the tree under which I can take my rest.
I like the thought of that
Because rest is unfamiliar right now,
And I could do with a bit of loving compensation.

The telephone has become my best friend,
A silent witness to our mutual torment.
You called me on my birthday to wish me happiness,
Giving your all,
A joyous three minute sound-bite of our life together.

On these May mornings filled with lilac promises,
Our dreams like wine still sleeping in the grape,
Clocks stand still until we can speak again,
Late at night when it's safe,
And you can call me wife without all hell breaking loose.

BEYOND REASON

For my darling Ahmed – always, yes to everything

I love you beyond reason,
Beyond seasons and summer rain,
Beyond fear, beyond pain.
I love you in the ocean's swell,
Beyond time, in ways I cannot tell.
I love you beyond light or trees,
Beyond grace or times of gentle ease.
I love you beyond silence,
Beyond hands that touch, or earth's own balance.
I love you beyond mind, or sight or song,
Beyond justice, far more than human right or wrong.
I love you beyond the endless path,
Beyond sun, stars, or eternal wrath.
I love you beyond home, or land, or castle's brick,
Beyond the chime of bells, or drum's dark tick.
I love you beyond heat or winter's frost,
Beyond treasure found, or youth that's long been lost.
I love you beyond brother, or the heart of any friend,
Beyond unwise beginnings, or Kismet's cruel bend.

I love you beyond tokens,
Beyond words spoken
Softly without thought,
Beyond battles fought.
I love you beyond rings or promises carved deep in stone,
Beyond dawn-fired hills which leave the soul undone.
I love you beyond joy, or grief, or loss or wealth,
Beyond poor body's need, or midnight's secret stealth.

I love you beyond the gilded face of faith's own cavalcade,
Beyond bold glory or any fleeting accolade.

I love you beyond order,
Beyond crossing borders
Or territorial sedition.
Beyond conditions.
I love you beyond learning,
Beyond passion's fire, beyond candles burning.
I love you beyond feasts and happy dance,
Beyond bud and bark, life's glittering glance.
I love you beyond the ancient written sacrament,
Beyond sword, or King, or heaven's spinning firmament.

I love you beyond growth, and Truth, and merry meeting,
Beyond departure, eventual return, and long-awaited greeting.

STILL
for all women 'of a certain age' everywhere

When I'm older,
Even older than today
And people tease me for my lack of crimplene suits and iron hair,
Waiting for that centennial 'gram to legitimise my life,
I'll still want to know
Everything...

I'll still smoke too many cigarettes,
Have all-night arguments where nobody gives an inch,
And the last word is the by-word for singularity of conversation.
I'll still wear black leather,
Show my Gothic cleavage
Bodiced so tight you could see my heart's blood-flow,
The Dark One silvering my mouth with his graciousness,
Proof positive that old vampires never die
Because they have a stake in eternity.

I'll still believe that beige should only ever be worn by camels,
That pink is for virgins,
That anything remotely pastel should be burned in Hell-fire,
Along with ALL cook books (yes burn, Delia, burn)
That life really IS too short to stuff a mushroom,
Especially when there's Salsa to kick
In red shoes high as steeples,
And I'm feeling keen as a mad dog biting.

I'll still flirt outrageously with pretty young men on buses,
Invite them home sometimes
For red wine and breakfast,

Show them my etchings,
Watch them dance naked in moonlight
Then demonstrate the right moves
Which, like riding a bicycle, a woman never forgets.

I'll still get drunk,
Fall out of telephone boxes; forget my name at parties because of
        Glenlivet's highland excess.
And I'll still sing rude songs
In the street at 3.00 a.m.,
With a rousing chorus that would have everything to do with body parts
        and midnight fantasies,
But nothing whatsoever to do with rugby, football, or any other game
Which only 'real men' can appreciate.

I'll still get turned on by the feel of silk on my skin,
Leopard spotted fake fur coats,
Mediterranean sun touching me,
Privately,
Like the lost lover who alone could bring me joy,
His kiss a faraway fickle wave-rush covering my mist-frosted shore,
The thought of his face still leaving me heart-scalded;
And if I lived to be a million it would never be finished.

I'll still travel in the desert,
See pyramids embroidered on lilac dim horizons,
Watch the dusk settle like a tired song over the sand dunes of
        Saqqara,
Come back from the Taklamakan like a fiery ghost,
Lose my shirt at Kashgar's Sunday market,
With the Uigar women,

Covered in fur and flowers,
Selling nomad trinkets,
Watching their men trade horses,
Shedding crescent moon smiles below Samarkand's blue mottled
        Registan,
And I'll still want the road to be endless.

Yea, when I'm older,
Even older than today,
And people who do not know me think I should be knitting or baking cakes,
Well, I'll still be laughing with Satan,
Covering my tracks with the Light of Heaven.

And I'll still want to know
Everything...

DIAMONDS

At a given moment
Not given,
Love dies.

I steel myself to loss,
All the sorrows of the world held at bay.
Wishing is not enough.
A dream is just a dream,
And days are a tightrope
Walked tremulously between waking and sleeping.
Sometimes all the sacrifice in the world
Is not enough.
The price is not always worth paying
And thus, cruelly,
Remains unpaid.

Regret crumbles
Like leaves rusting in September's fingers.
The damaged heart keens in unvoiced desolation
Silent as trees at leaf death.

At a given moment,
Written but not given,
Love dies.

You were to me like diamonds.

QUANTUM LOVE

When, alone, you stand in shifting circles of wine and silence,
Your lover across the room, lifting the glass to his lips while you taste
    the tandem grape;
Or, in land-locked oceans, he swims,
Deaf to the echoes of ancient whale-song,
Yet, hearing your breath, in-take matching out-take,
Knowing the perfect pulse without missing a beat;
And you stretch out your hand, while he,
Across continents,
Feels that touch upon his skin;
Even, when strafing mental nebulae, or riding the cosmic slipstream,
You laugh with simultaneous diversion,
Action and reaction in synchronised momentum,
Then, you know,
You've got
Quantum love.

When he opens the door, and you step through it,
Linear time together a nonsense in your non-locality loving,
And everything you are, or were, or will be
Happens simultaneously,
Each act a constant, challenging accepted laws of physics,
Your universe no ultra-violet catastrophe of the heart,
But a changing room of non-variable paradox,
Your neutron, his proton, joined in sub-atomic spin.
Yea...
You've got
Quantum love.

When, whatever you do,
You do,
You do,
And do,
Repeated, repeated, sated, completed,
Both beginning and end,
Or anywhere between,
Alive to exactly the same point of time or space
Continuously,
And words rush from mouth to ear with no time spent on travel,
Future and past joined forever in the present,
For sure,
You've got
Quantum love.

Outside of chaos theory,
Your teardrop creates no tidal wave of passion,
But births all possibilities in parallel,
Shifting and harmonic,
Mechanical variations making no difference at all.
And how you live in your world
Is a reflection of the world you live in.
The pain you feel is always felt,
The joy you know is always known,
You and he and she and them and us in endless permutation.
And if you cannot kiss him today,
Know that first kiss is still,
Still happening in the eternal present,
For we
Are talking
Quantum love.

Her hair was like rivers, like whirlpools,
A lake at sunset soft wave a-ripple, all edged in memories of Russia.

Her hair was like China silk, glinting with dragon's eyes,
Or velvet from Venice, where Doge's float amidst the glass and gilded
    statuettes.

Her hair was like autumn, like blackberries, like rooks calling,
And apple-fire burning surrounding you with warmth and safety.

Her hair smelled of hibiscus, rosemary, sweet columbine,
A supple bed of herbal resolution where you could lay, certain of comfort.

Her hair was like Zen, a mantra,
Oohm-oohm of Buddha's breathe, serenity hidden,
The eyes of the faithful when called to God's grace.

Her hair was like tragedy, an endless shriek, black despair,
As if you had lost in love a thousand times,
Soul laid bare to wounds that can never heal, and pain that will never
    cease.

Her hair smelled of pinewoods and palm trees, of lemon zest and lilac,
Of making love amongst brambles, thorns marking nakedness,
Piercing you awake as dusk settled like bruising, and the world became
    still.

Her hair was like serpents, a chequered nest of vipers,
Diamonds of colour scaling sinuous writhing wrapped round your throat
    with blemishing grip,

Bite sharp enough to snatch your life.

Her hair was like wheat fields, rolling and rustling without digression,
Carpeting stems bent heavy to the ground,
Uniting earth to growth, eyeless and swaying.

Her hair was like cobwebs, whispering cross your face in sleep,
The most tenuous of touching, feet of spiders,
Each tendril a dew-filled trap in which you crouch, like a struggling fly.

Her hair was like ladders, like falling, plummeting from sky to rocks
To the bare earth filled with the bones of broken things,
Men who had loved unwisely,
I who had loved unwisely,
Giving myself unwisely to ease her escape,
Falling and dreaming, unwisely,
Falling and dreaming...
                    unwisely.

Her hair was like dreaming, an ivory tower glimpsed,
A call of faithlessness, shifting and tumbling.

Her hair was like snowfall, muting the landscape, covering it
        with a clean embrace.

Her hair was like holding, a blanket of graciousness; a perfect chord
        in the ear.

Her hair was a promise, a testimony; a pledge of better things.

Her hair was forever.

BACK IN BODRUM (2 - 5May)

I had forgotten geraniums could shout so scarlet.
That on May mornings the Aegean is no longer a sword.
That sparrows can flicker over water,
Eyes bright with challenge,
Leaving holes with each tiny mouthful snatched.

And I remember that palm trees speak to each other secretly,
Congregating at roadsides to rustle up mischief,
While pines drone in dark green descant.

IN MY HEAVEN

In my heaven, God rides a Harley,
650cc, heavy duty,
Chrome and mirrors everywhere.
He has snakeskin boots with silver spurs
To let you know He's there,
Black leathers (with no 'give' at all),
A tattoo saying 'Jesus Saves - and so do I'
Surrounded by serpents,
In red
Upon His back.

No harps in my heaven,
Or haloed creatures
Bent on unremitting choral song,
Or cherubs wreathed in rosebuds
Garlanded in bland celestial smiles.

In my heaven, the angels wear Armani jackets
Cut to hide the feathers,
Versace suits, serious Gucci shades...
They smell of 'Eternity' by Calvin Klein.

Michael wields his rod of fire to Johnny Whitehill,
Hooker, deep in cosmic rhythm, tapping his feet,
BB the only King worth listening to.

In my heaven, there are no doctors.
An apple a day has kept them all
Out.

At the gate, Peter's all tooled up to keep away the riff-raff,
His gold chain of office direct from Cartier,
A diamond in his ear the size of Paris.

No virgins in my heaven,
No-one who has not swallowed Ecstasy
Whole,
Then kept on dancing,
God rapping on the bar with His long, hard fingers,
Challenging you with that Almighty smile,
Buying you a Bud.

In my heaven, reality is virtual, not virtuous,
Transportation something that lets you cross the hallowed streets of
        Paradise
Untouched.
Atonement's not a word in my divine vocabulary,
Nothing original about my sin,
The body of evidence getting
Very
Very
Physical.

SNAKE

Poetry is a snake,
Words curled under rocks and stones,
Round the base of trees, helixed in hubcaps,
Waiting to strike.
And every time I'm just about ready to give it up,
Plagued by self-doubt,
Weary of relentless word-fit and betrayal...
I get bitten.

And poetry is an illusive song drifting over rain and ridges,
Lao Tzu – the way,
Torn through mountains bristling with eagles and wild dogs,
A beckoning horizon,
A laughing oasis,
A homecoming,
A comfortable bed at the end of a long journey,
To sleep at last after so much restless wandering,
Golden apple dreaming,
A fierce tempest,
A quiet haven after the storm where boats are resting
Ragged and torn, tired, for now, of the sea's kiss.

And poetry is a battle,
A sword thrust, deep and fatal,
A healing,
A forest,
A full meal to a beggar coming in from winter for warmth and feasting,
Hope re-kindled, voice re-found,
So that he can speak his name again, without shame.

And poetry is a predator with sharp teeth and claws,
Theasaurus Rex,
Aroused and waiting,
Greedy for your heart, alive and palpitating in its mouth,
A demon at midnight,
A jealous mistress,
A whore,
Whipping you on with her terrible wounding love,
A debt-collector, taxing your soul,
Taking everything,
Leaving nothing behind;
The lover who torments you,
Each kiss a sharp retreat.

And poetry is a lonely tower,
The ghost at the feast,
An iron wall keeping you separate,
Beguiling you with soft promises,
Star song,
Plain chant,
Drum and pipe,
As if all the creatures of heaven were chorusing at your window,
As if Lucifer himself in all his peacock glory had entered you,
Through invitation,
Knowing your name,
Laying his hand upon you openly,
A lost boy,
A dark angel,
Piercing you with his stone-dead eyes,
Blue as dawn's first light.

Oh, poetry is a snake,
The Tree of Life,
With Adam and Eve on their knees outside the Gates of Paradise,
Eternal worm,
Oroboros, consuming itself,
Start and end,
The circle,
Fire in the sky,
Sun and Moon captivated in rhythm,
Serpent, carrying the universe
Carrying me on its back
Like a child, an acolyte,
A pagan dance,
The Mother,
Full circle.
A snake.

Thank you for buying *Woman*. Agnes Meadows is fabulously well-travelled poet and workshop leader. She also runs Loose Muse, a reading series for women writers of all genres. You can follow her work and projects online at:

http://loose-muse.com/
and on twitter at: @AgnesMeadows1

—§—

flipped eye publishing is dedicated to publishing powerful new voices in affordable volumes. Founded in 2001, we have won awards and international recognition through our focus on publishing fiction and poetry that is clear and true, rather than exhibitionist.

If you would like more information about flipped eye publishing, please join our mailing list online at **www.flippedeye.net**.

Lightning Source UK Ltd.
Milton Keynes UK
UKHW010721210321
380690UK00002B/92